THE LOVE TUNE-UP

How To Amp Up the Love That's Naturally Inside
You To Have Happy, Healthy Relationships

— A 14-Day Course That Can Change Your Life —

THE LOVE TUNE-UP

How To Amp Up the Love That's Naturally Inside
You To Have Happy, Healthy Relationships

— A 14-Day Course That Can Change Your Life —

Dr. Suzanne J. Gelb, Ph.D., J.D.

FIRST EDITION

All rights reserved. This book or any portion thereof may not be reproduced or used in any manner whatsoever without the express written permission of the publisher except for the use of brief quotations in a book review.

Copyright © 2019 Dr. Suzanne J. Gelb, Ph.D., J.D.

Manufactured in the United States of America.

ISBN-13: 978-1-950764-01-3
ISBN-10: 1-950764-01-X

www.DrSuzanneGelb.com

PRAISE FOR... THE LOVE TUNE-UP

What Readers Are Saying

"We loved all 14 lessons. Packed with information and tips. It took our relationship to the next level and improved our lives, individually."

— Cheryl and Tim (married for three years)

"*This saved our relationship and was just what we needed to shift from considering splitting up to being a success story. Thank you, thank you.*"

— Joe and Maxine (dating for a year)

"I'm single and hope to meet 'the one' soon. The Love Tune-Up opened my eyes to many things about relationships — with myself and my soon-to-be significant other (fingers crossed!).

I feel much more confident about dating now, and I don't feel like I used to about relationships… like they're a gamble and you never know if they're going to work out long-term. After doing this course, I know that I'm on strong ground with a relationship as long as I have a strong relationship with myself."

— BW (single)

DEDICATION

Tune up your car.

Tune up your guitar.

And now... tune up your heart.

The Love Tune-Up is a course dedicated to people who love... love.

(And want to do it right).

CONTENTS

Disclaimer — xv

INTRODUCTION

Fine-Tune Your Relationship With Yourself, Fine-Tune Your Relationship With Others. — 1

CHAPTER 1

The 3 Elements of a Happy, Loving Relationship. — 7

CHAPTER 2

3 Love-Sabotaging Habits That Must Go. — 11

CHAPTER 3

3 Truths About What Makes a Relationship "Work." — 15

CHAPTER 4

Reflecting on What You've Learned So Far. — 18

CHAPTER 5

Tuning Up Your ... Ability to Be the Real You. — 21

CHAPTER 6

Tuning Up Your ... Ability to Be a Good Listener. — 23

CHAPTER 7

Tuning Up Your ... Ability to Compromise.　　26

CHAPTER 8

Tuning Up Your ... Ability To Be Flexible.　　30

CHAPTER 9

Tuning Up Your ... Ability to Forgive and Let Go of Resentment.　　33

CHAPTER 10

Tuning Up Your ... Ability To Release Anger Safely and Keep the Peace.　　36

CHAPTER 11

Tuning Up Your ... Self-Love.　　39

CHAPTER 12

Tuning Up Your ... Self-Respect.　　42

CHAPTER 13

Tuning Up Your ... Gratitude.　　45

CHAPTER 14

A Few Words of Encouragement.　　48

WRAP UP

Resources… To Keep the Love Rolling.   50

WHAT'S NEXT?

Remembering to Tune-Up Your Relationship with Yourself and / or Your Partner.   67

HAPPINESS BEGINS NOW: CREATING YOUR TRULY EXCEPTIONAL LIFE ONE STEP AT A TIME.   70

MORE TIPS, MORE TOOLS

FAQs About How To Find Love — and Stay in Love.   72

ABOUT THE AUTHOR   95

OTHER BOOKS BY THE AUTHOR   96

INDEX   98

DISCLAIMER

This book is a tool that can help you build relationships that really work — by improving the most important relationship of all: your relationship with yourself.

This book contains educational exercises and tips drawn from my career in the field of emotional wellness with over 30 years of experience. This book is for informational purposes only, and is not intended to diagnose or treat any illness, nor is it a substitute for professional or psychological advice, diagnosis, or treatment. Always consult a qualified health care professional before engaging in any new, self-help resource (such as this one) and with questions you may have about your health and wellbeing.

Any case material that may be indirectly alluded to in this book, in articles, or in interviews [see Resources section] does not constitute guarantees of similar outcomes for the reader. No results can be promised, since everyone's personal development path is unique.

Links inside this book to external websites are for informational purposes only. Linking does not imply endorsement of or affiliation with that site, its content, or any product or service it may offer.

All link URLs in this book are current at the time of printing. Link URLs may fail at some point if the page has been deleted or moved. The author assumes no responsibility or liability for broken links.

This concludes the disclaimer portion of this book.

Enjoy *The Love Tune-Up*. Here's to love.

INTRODUCTION

Fine-Tune Your Relationship With Yourself, Fine-Tune Your Relationships With Others

Hello and Welcome:

I'm Dr. Suzanne Gelb, Ph.D., J.D., a psychologist, life coach and relationship expert.

I've spent thousands of hours over the past 30+ years, helping men, women and couples, to successfully optimize and upgrade their relationships, using tools like the ones you'll learn about in this book.

Helping people to find love — and stay in love — is one of my absolute favorite things in the world.

May I Offer You... a Tune-Up:

Everything in the world needs a tune-up, from time to time.

You tune-up your guitar. You tune-up your car. You re-boot your computer and update your programs. You tune-up your career, based on feedback from your latest review, or a request from your boss.

It's always good to check-in and recharge, making sure you're on the right track.

But when it comes to our **relationships?**

Many of us forget — or, don't want — to check-in.

And many of us avoid doing a tune-up... until things have already gotten really bad.

But it doesn't have to be that way.

Especially, not after today.

Because today... you've chosen to dive into this course called *The Love Tune-Up.*

(Congratulations!)

Recognizing That You Might Need a "Tune-Up" in the Love Department Does Not Mean That You're "Messed Up" or "Broken":

It just means that you recognize that there is room for improvement. That is a beautiful, commendable thing.

By choosing to give yourself a tune-up with this course, you'll be joining many others who have learned how to start having happy, healthy relationships, and I am wishing you tremendous success.

Choose Love — and you'll always be on the right track.

Why Did Dr. Gelb Create This Course:

Because I believe that Love is our natural state.

Love is how we were born. Love is where we belong. Being loving is what we naturally want to do. You don't have to force it. But… you might need to make a few shifts and adjustments to return back home. Back to your natural state. Back to Love.

Just like re-aligning the tires of your car… or re-stringing a guitar… **a little tune-up can go a long way.**

So, enjoy *The Love Tune-Up* as you commit to creating a more loving relationship with yourself… and with others.

Loving Ourselves, Loving Others, and Being Loved Should Be Simple — and Yet, for Many People, It's Not That Way:

That's another reason why I created this course: to make things simple. And hopefully, to make it a little easier for you to start to receive the love you deserve. From yourself. And from others.

The Love Tune-Up reflects my many years of work in the emotional wellness field. I've poured my heart — and experience — into this clear, simple program.

I hope it is uplifting and useful to you.

You Set the Tone for all of the Relationships in Your Life:

"Why can't I meet someone amazing? I feel like I'm never going to meet The One..."

"What happened to my relationship? It used to be sexy and exciting, but now? Ugh..."

"Why does my partner drive me so crazy? I try to keep my cool, but he / she just pushes all of my buttons..."

"Why are relationships just so HARD! I wish I could feel happy and relaxed and... in love, you know?"

Those who are asking these types of questions and look **Inward** for answers, are far more likely to learn to build successful relationships and achieve their relationship goals — than those who look **Outward**. True Love starts within.

When we love and respect ourselves, we tend to form relationships with people who love and respect us, too.

Makes sense. Totally true. But... not always easy to do.

If you're having a tough time "loving" yourself — or even "liking" yourself, sometimes — *The Love Tune-Up* teaches you how to start being kinder to yourself. By the time you finish, you can be on your way to being more self-loving and self-respecting — the building blocks to positive relationships.

How The Love Tune-Up Works:

The Love Tune-Up is a course for those who want to learn how to build relationships that really work.

Here are 3 things to know:

1. The overall **philosophy** of *The Love Tune-Up* is this:

In order to create the relationship of your dreams with another person, first, you need to create the relationship of your dreams with yourself.

2. It doesn't matter if you're currently **single** (and not looking for a partner), **single** (and definitely looking for a partner), or part of a **couple**. The lessons in *The Love Tune-Up* can work for all 3 situations.

3. *The Love Tune-Up* is **14 days long**. You have access to all the love lessons right here — so you can go at your own pace. Ideally, complete one short love lesson each day. Some lessons will involve journaling, others will invite you to try out a new self-care practice, express yourself openly in a conversation, or even go on a date!

There's no "expiration date" on *The Love Tune-Up*, and you can begin the course any time that you like. There's no pressure and no rush. But… why wait? It's always the right time to choose Love.

Tired of Relationships That Just... Don't... Work:

My highest hope is that this course can inspire you to become a happier, more self-loving person, regardless of whether you're currently in a relationship — or seeking one.

Because happy, self-loving people build happy, loving relationships ... naturally.

Here's to love.

Day 1 of your tune-up is next.

CHAPTER 1

The 3 Elements of a Happy, Loving Relationship

Welcome to Day 1 of The Love Tune-Up.

Your love lesson of the day?

The 3 Elements of a Happy, Loving Relationship.

These elements have been successfully incorporated into thousands of hours of helping individuals and couples who have visited my office.

The relationships that really work — and stand the test of time — always embrace these 3 elements. The relationships that don't work ... do not!

Read on, and then pop down to the very end of this lesson for your **Tune-Up of the Day**.

1. Be the Real You.

So many of us behave in a way that we think will please others.

We're afraid of not being "liked" or "accepted" so we hide our true colors.

But if you try to be someone you're not, it will backfire sooner or later. And you'll never be satisfied in a relationship, because your partner won't have gotten the chance to know and connect with the real you.

In order to build a happy, loving relationship, you must be your true self.

2. Be a Good Listener.

When you listen, you're showing respect for the person who is speaking, even if you disagree with what's being said.

In a sense, you're saying, *"I'm interested in what you have to say. I love you and I care enough to give you my full attention."*

Your partner, in turn, feels validated and understood.

Good listening skills include maintaining eye contact when someone is speaking to you, giving your partner your undivided attention (not tapping away on your phone), and listening patiently while letting the other person finish talking.

In order to build a happy, loving relationship, you must be willing to listen.

3. Be Open To Compromise.

Compromising doesn't mean that you are "weak".

It means that you're courageous enough to give up something, if that's what's best for your relationship. It's about diverting potential conflict, instead of letting problems fester.

In order to build a happy, loving relationship, you must be willing to compromise.

Your Tune-Up of the Day:

If you're single: Looking at your last relationship, which of these elements was very strong? Which was the weakest?

If you're part of a couple: Looking at your current relationship, which of these elements are very strong? Which is the weakest?

Whichever element is the weakest, say out loud to yourself:

"I recognize that _____ is essential in order to build a happy, loving relationship. I am making a commitment, right now, to make it a priority."

If you'd like to do a little more tuning-up, **do some journaling** at the end of your day.

Write down three ways that you made _____ a priority, today.

If you weren't able to make _____ a priority, write down why you weren't able to do it.

This writing process can lead to more insights about yourself, and how you live and love.

This wraps up Day 1 of The Love Tune-Up.

I'll "see " you tomorrow, to talk about ... The 3 Love-Sabotaging Habits That Must Go.

CHAPTER 2

3 Love-Sabotaging Habits That Must Go

Welcome to Day 2 of The Love Tune-Up.

Your love lesson of the day?

3 Love-Sabotaging Habits That Must Go.

Oof! These negative habits can be serious relationship-wreckers — not just for romantic relationships and partnerships, but for relationships with friends, family and co-workers. Not to mention … your relationship with yourself.

But once you're aware of them, you can take steps to resolve them.

Read on, and then pop down to the very end of this lesson for your **Tune-Up of the Day**.

1. Trying to "Make" Someone Change.

You can support your partner in making positive life choices. You can celebrate their successes. You can express your own hopes and dreams. But ultimately, you can't "make" someone change.

Real change comes from within — from a personal desire to transform, not from external pressure.

Trying to "make" someone become the person that YOU want them to be is a huge source of tension for so many couples. It just doesn't work.

And conversely, nobody can "make" you change, either! Inspiration can come from the outside world and the people around you, but only you can choose to change and grow.

2. Holding Onto Resentment.

Holding onto a "grudge" is painful for you. It can also be painful for the person you won't forgive.

For a relationship to work, forgiveness is a necessary component.

Forgiving someone doesn't mean that what the other person did was "OK" or that it's fine if they do it again. It just means that you're willing to move on and let go of the emotional baggage, so that the relationship can have a chance to mend.

Not being able to forgive other people is painful, but not being able to forgive yourself is painful, too! To create a happy, healthy relationship with yourself, it's vital that you forgive yourself for past mistakes and don't treat yourself like a "failure" or "the enemy".

3. Blowing Up With Anger.

If you don't know how to manage your stress levels, you might very well blow up in anger.

Pent-up anger usually comes out, one way or another — sometimes, by verbally lashing out at the one you love and sometimes, by sabotaging yourself (think: anger turned inward).

Anger turned inward can look like: bingeing on ice cream, sabotaging your chances for a promotion at work, or canceling a date with a terrific person at the last moment, because you're disappointed with yourself or just feeling plain down.

It's essential to learn how to release pent-up anger safely and in private — by pounding a pillow with a hand-towel that's been knotted on one end, for example — and simultaneously, verbalizing how you feel.

Your Tune-Up of the Day:

Which of these love-sabotaging habits have you noticed yourself doing? (Even just "occasionally".)

Be honest, and say out loud to yourself:

"I recognize that _____ is a negative habit. It is interfering with my ability to love, and be loved.

I am making a commitment, right now, to manage my emotions in a healthier way so that I can stop doing it."

(And don't worry … we'll talk about how to "manage your emotions" all throughout this course. By the end, you may just feel like a pro!)

This wraps up Day 2 of The Love Tune-Up.

Tomorrow, we'll walk through … 3 Truths About What Makes A Relationship "Work".

CHAPTER **3**

3 Truths About What Makes a Relationship "Work"

Welcome to Day 3 of The Love Tune-Up.

Your love lesson of the day?

3 Truths About What Makes a Relationship "Work".

There's so much uncertainty about what makes a relationship "work".

But the truth is … it's not actually that complicated.

These "truths" may initially seem geared towards people who are in a relationship with someone, or looking to be in a relationship, but at the end of the day, these truths apply to your relationship with yourself, as well.

Read on, and then pop down to the very end of this lesson for your **Tune-Up of the Day**.

1. It Takes Two Emotionally-Whole People To Make a Relationship "Work".

Otherwise, if one or both people are emotionally needy — they may look to the other to fill emotional voids that they need to fill for themselves.

2. Respect Is Essential.

In order to form and sustain a happy relationship, there needs to be a foundation of genuine admiration and respect, flowing both ways.

Of course, if you don't admire and respect yourself, it's very tough to admire and respect someone else.

3. People Who Feel Good About Themselves Have Happy Relationships.

A person who feels good about themselves (aka: is self-loving) wouldn't get involved in a relationship that's unhealthy and unsatisfying.

A person who feels good about themselves wouldn't be attracted to someone whose behavior is unkind.

When we feel good about ourselves, we feel worthy of being treated with kindness and sensitivity. And that's exactly what we seek out and attract.

Our relationships reflect, to one degree or another, how we feel about ourselves.

So, if you want to meet someone and form a happy relationship, or you want the relationship you're in to be happier, the first step is to commit to feeling good about "you", which means loving yourself more ... right now. Self-love changes everything.

Your Tune-Up of the Day:

Take a short, but powerful **self-love inventory**:

- Do I treat myself with kindness and sensitivity?

- Do I accept my strengths and limitations (things I'm not good at or haven't mastered yet)?

- Can I genuinely say, *"I admire and respect myself"*?

- If a partner said to me, *"You're a wonderful person..."* would I believe them?

Once you've answered these questions, take a moment to give yourself a big hug.

No matter how much (or how little) you love yourself today, you can love yourself even more.

This wraps up Day 3 of The Love Tune-Up.

Next lesson? A little check-in so you can seamlessly integrate everything you've learned so far.

CHAPTER 4

Reflecting on What You've Learned So Far

Welcome to Day 4 of The Love Tune-Up.

Today, take a breather. Literally: take a nice, full, deep breath.

Then, take some time to reflect on your first few lessons and think about what you've learned about yourself so far.

To recap, here's what's we've "talked" about …

The 3 Elements of a Happy, Loving Relationship.

1. Be the real you.

2. Be a good listener.

3. Be open to compromise.

3 Love-Sabotaging Habits That Must Go.

1. Trying to "make" someone change.

2. Holding onto resentment.

3. Blowing up with anger.

3 Truths About What Makes a Relationship "Work".

1. It takes two emotionally-whole people to make a relationship "work".

2. Respect is essential.

3. People who feel good about themselves have happy relationships.

Your Tune-Up of the Day:

Based on what you've learned so far, **complete the following statement** (either in writing or out loud):

"When it comes to feeling good about myself and taking great care of myself, I'm realizing that _____ is one area that could use a tune-up.

I will focus on that for the rest of the day."

This wraps up Day 4 of The Love Tune-Up.

I'll "see" you tomorrow for a love lesson on … how to express your true self.

Chapter 5

Tuning Up Your ... Ability To Be the Real You

Welcome to Day 5 of The Love Tune-Up.

Today, we're going to focus on **tuning up your ... authenticity!**

Remember back on Day 1 of **The Love Tune-Up**, being the real you was identified as one of the 3 elements of a happy, loving relationship. (The very first one, in fact!)

But what does it mean to "be your true self"? How can you learn to be "the real you" more effortlessly, if you've been disconnected from your real self for a very long time ... as so many people are?

You Can Start With a Mini Self-Evaluation.

Ask yourself:

- Am I honest and open in relationships, or do I hold back because I'm worried about what others may think?

- Is there a dream I haven't pursued because I'm afraid that people won't like me if they see my true colors? (Or, if I don't succeed.)

- What am I afraid of, more than anything in the world?

Once you have written down your answers, take a moment to soothe any fears you may have, by comforting your inner child — the child that you once were. This is typically the root source of our fears ... and the part of us that invariably needs some extra love.

How To Comfort Your Inner Child:

Sit comfortably. Place a pillow on your lap. Now, close your eyes and picture yourself having a conversation with another person.

Notice how fear may be stopping you from sharing your real self... sharing what you truly think and feel.

Then hold the pillow close to you, as if you're tenderly holding the child you once were, that part of you that's scared.

This wraps up Day 5 of The Love Tune-Up.

I'll "see" you tomorrow for a love lesson on ... listening.

CHAPTER **6**

Tuning Up Your ... Ability To Be a Good Listener

Welcome to Day 6 of The Love Tune-Up.

Today, we're going to focus on **tuning up your ... listening skills.**

Listening seems like it would be "easy". After all, what could be simpler than just sitting ... while someone else speaks ... hearing their words ... saying nothing?

But when it comes to listening, there are some definite behaviors to avoid, yet so many people engage in these No-No's.

So, how are your listening skills? Let's find out!

Here's a List of 'What Not To Do' When You're Listening:

DON'T:

- Interrupt when someone else is speaking.

- Finish other people's sentences.

- Cut people off or change subjects.

- Overreact and jump to conclusions (pause, breathe, think — before you speak).

- Mind-read or make assumptions about what the other person is trying to say.

- Allow your own biases to block your ability to listen with an open mind.

- Give unsolicited advice.

- Monopolize the conversation by repeatedly shifting the focus to yourself.

- Pretend to listen when in fact you're rehearsing what you're going to say.

- Engage in selective listening (i.e., listening to only parts of the conversation).

Your Tune-Up of the Day:

Ask yourself:

- Do any of the behaviors listed above apply to me?

- Which ones?

Make a commitment to **become more aware**, in those moments when you're slipping into "bad listening habits".

Then, tonight, curl up with a cup of tea (or warm beverage of your choice) and **do some journaling**.

Write about what it felt like to listen actively and deeply — with a partner, on a date, with a colleague, or even with a customer service representative over the phone.

If you had a tough time listening, write about that. Reflect on why that might be happening — where you might have picked up some "bad listening habits" and why you have a tendency to engage in them.

This wraps up Day 6 of The Love Tune-Up.

I'll "see" you tomorrow for a love lesson on ... compromising.

CHAPTER **7**

Tuning Up Your ... Ability To Compromise

Welcome to Day 7 of The Love Tune-Up.

Today, we're going to focus on **tuning up your ... ability to compromise.**

This is a must for your relationship tool kit — a potent way to handle potential conflict.

But so many people resist this problem-diverter.

They misunderstand compromise.

They have the wrong impression of it.

Yes, it may involve you and / or your partner giving up something you want ... but for a good reason: to settle your differences.

Let's Clear up Some Myths About Compromise:

- It doesn't mean that you're letting someone walk all over you.

- It doesn't mean that someone else is right and you're wrong.

- It doesn't mean that someone else wins and you lose.

- It doesn't mean that someone else is strong and you're weak and passive.

- It doesn't mean that you're denying your "true self".

Compromise is really about doing what's best for your relationship — which means a win-win for you (when your relationship benefits, you do too!)

Your Tune-Up of the Day:

Write down your answers to these 3 questions:

1. When you hear the word "compromise", how do you feel? How about a "peace-keeping choice"? Or a "self-respecting choice"? Or simply "healthy behavior"?

2. Do you feel comfortable making compromises in your relationships? If not, why not?

3. After you make a compromise, do you feel resentful and angry? If so, describe how that feels.

Now that you have some insight into how you handle compromise, take a few minutes to **reflect on healthy compromise** — and what that feels like.

A 5-Minute Reflection.

Sit comfortably or lie down. Close your eyes and take a deep breath.

As you breathe in, think, "When I compromise, I am being respectful to myself and others."

As you exhale, imagine you're releasing any resentment or anger.

Breathe in. Now imagine you're breathing in love and respect.

As you exhale, again, imagine you're releasing any resentment and anger.

One more time, breathe in love and respect.

As you exhale, imagine yourself feeling comfortable with compromise.

Now, still with your eyes closed, we'll repeat this exercise two more times and you can feel how your attitude about compromise may start to shift.

And when you're ready, you can slowly begin to open your eyes and adjust to the light in your environment... feeling calm, comfortable and strong.

And so it is!

This wraps up Day 7 of The Love Tune-Up.

I'll "see" you tomorrow for a love lesson on … flexibility and letting go of expectations.

Chapter 8

Tuning Up Your ... Ability To Be Flexible

Welcome to Day 8 of The Love Tune-Up.

Today, we're going to work on tuning up your ... ability to be flexible and let go of expectations.

As Alexander Pope once wrote:

"Blessed is he who expects nothing, for he shall never be disappointed."

I love it when people have high goals, standards and dreams ... and a lot of hope.

But we run into problems when we expect people, or life, to measure up to our standards. People have free choice — they won't always behave the way we'd like.

Life is a gamble — things may not always go the way we want.

And when what we expect doesn't happen, we often feel angry — instantly.

But we can learn to let go of expecting people to behave a certain way, or that life will work out in a certain way — while still holding onto lots of hope!

Start by Answering the Following Questions:

- When you're dating someone — or in a committed relationship — do you get annoyed if you ask your partner to change their behavior, but they don't do it?

- Do you get frustrated because your partner doesn't share all of your interests and opinions, or get along with all of your friends?

- Do you get irritated when people don't behave the way you think they should?

- Does your annoyance, frustration or irritation sometimes linger for a while and bring you down?

If you answered "Yes" to any of these questions, consider letting go of expectations and saying "hello" to greater happiness.

Your Tune-Up of the Day:

Today, **pick one (or more) of the affirmations** below and **set a timer** to prompt you to **say them out loud**, every hour:

- *I let go of expecting others to behave in a certain way.*

- *I let go of the need to change others, in order to satisfy my emotional needs.*

- *I take responsibility for satisfying my own emotional needs.*

- *I give myself all the love, support and direction I need.*

- *I recognize that no one is perfect. (And that includes me.)*

When you say — and believe — these words, it is an **act of love for yourself and others**.

When love is present, there is little room for expectations.

This wraps up Day 8 of The Love Tune-Up.

Next Up. A love lesson on … forgiveness and letting go of resentment.

CHAPTER 9

Tuning Up Your ... Ability to Forgive and Let Go of Resentment

Welcome to Day 9 of The Love Tune-Up.

Today, we're going to focus on tuning up your ... **ability to forgive and let go of resentment.**

If you resent someone for how they treated you in the past, you're probably paying a big price for feeling this way. You may be so consumed with resentment that you cannot enjoy the present moment.

Being burdened with resentment is a miserable way to move through life. And people who feel miserable do not form happy, whole-hearted relationships. That's another big price you're paying.

Learning to forgive someone is not a sign of weakness. It's just the opposite. It is a sign of strength. A sign of healing.

As Dr. Wayne Dyer said:

"… perhaps the most healing thing that you can do [is] to remove the low energies of resentment and revenge from your life completely."

Your Tune-Up of the Day:

Today, write a letter to someone towards whom you feel resentful or angry.

This letter will <u>never</u> be sent, but it can give you a chance to **safely express your feelings**.

Don't worry about spelling, grammar or punctuation. In your letter, tell that person how hurt or disappointed you feel by what they did — and what you want them to say or do to make things right.

Then, tear the letter up. While doing so, talk out loud and "tell" the person you resent how you feel (make sure you have privacy). Don't hold back — let your feelings out.

Once you've released your feelings, so that they are no longer "smoldering" inside, **you may feel more ready to forgive.**

Try saying out loud:

[Person's name], I forgive you for [name the behavior that you resent].

This doesn't mean that what you did was OK, or that you can do it again.

Still, I forgive you.

Because I deserve to have a happy and healthy life, without being emotionally burdened.

I forgive you, because I am ready to move on.

If you still feel angry, you may need to release more anger, in a deeper way — in private. Consider pounding a pillow using a hand-towel that's been knotted on one end and at the same time, verbalizing how you feel; or you may want to consult a qualified professional.

This wraps up Day 9 of The Love Tune-Up.

I'll see you tomorrow for a love lesson on … Keeping the peace.

CHAPTER 10

Tuning Up Your ... Ability To Release Anger Safely and Keep the Peace

Welcome to Day 10 of The Love Tune-Up.

Today, we're going to focus on **tuning up your ... ability to release anger safely and keep the peace**.

You might not think of yourself as an "angry person", but keep in mind: holding onto anger doesn't always look like yelling, screaming, or an explosive, hostile outburst.

- Are you ever "hostile" towards others in less dramatic, but equally blistering ways — by speaking in a snarky tone of voice, belittling other people's ideas, or punishing your partner in a "passive-aggressive" way, for example?

- Are you ever "hostile" towards yourself in less dramatic, but equally blistering ways as well — by speaking to yourself in a cruel way, or neglecting to take loving, respectful care of your body, for example?

To relate more peacefully towards others — and to make peace with yourself — you would need to know how to manage your anger safely and appropriately.

Your Tune-Up of the Day:

Today, find a way to **safely release your anger**, in private.

You might try …

- Pounding a pillow (using a towel that you've knotted on one end) while venting your feelings out loud.

- Yelling into a pillow (it muffles the sound).

- Doing some journaling and then tearing up the paper.

If you're thinking, "But I'm not angry right now..." that's OK. You can still do one of these exercises, if you'd like. Just think about the last time you felt angry and begin doing an exercise. At first, you might just go through the motions. But if the anger's still inside you (it's just been suppressed), the emotion is likely to resurface, as you continue the exercise.

After releasing your anger, **write about how you feel**. Read over what you wrote and then write some more, if you want to. When you're finished, shred your writing or burn it. Do this to ensure privacy and also as another way of releasing the angry feelings.

This wraps up Day 10 of The Love Tune-Up.

I'll "see" you tomorrow for a love lesson on … self-love.

CHAPTER 11

Tuning Up Your ... Self-Love

Welcome to Day 11 of The Love Tune-Up.

Today, we're going to focus on **tuning up your ... self-love**.

Think about your relationship with yourself. How you talk to yourself. How you treat yourself. The expectations you set for yourself.

Would you describe your relationship with yourself as ...

Impatient. Unkind. Unfair. Dishonest. Disrespectful. Distrustful.

Or ... loving?

If you feel that your relationship with yourself is less loving than it could be, it can be useful to explore why that might be.

- Are you engaging in unloving behaviors that you learned as a child?

- Are you experiencing something more current — stemming from a recent disappointment or heartbreak that you haven't resolved yet.

If you're not sure where it's all coming from, that's OK, too.

It is possible to learn to be more self-loving, regardless of whether or not you know exactly why you haven't been loving in the past.

Your Tune-Up of the Day:

Today, you have an opportunity to **make a promise to be more self-loving.**

To make it official, **we'll put this promise in a contract that you'll find on the next page** — one of the most important contracts you'll ever sign.

My Love Contract

I, _____, promise to be patient, kind, fair and honest with myself.

I will respect, listen, accept and trust myself.

I have not always treated myself with love in the past, and I forgive myself fully for that.

As of this moment, I commit to a life of love.

Signed: _____ Date: _____

Write this contract on a separate piece of pager.

Then…

Sign and date this contract and post it in an area where you'll see it often — on your bathroom mirror, on your fridge, or tucked in the front of your evening journal.

Read this contract out loud at least 3 times today. Imagine that you're reading it to the child who you once were, or even the person you were, yesterday … assuring that "earlier self" that things are different, now.

This wraps up Day 11 of The Love Tune-Up.

I'll "see" you tomorrow for a love lesson on … self-respect.

CHAPTER 12

Tuning Up Your ... Self-Respect

Welcome to Day 12 of The Love Tune-Up.

Today, we're going to focus on **tuning up your ... self-respect.**

What does being "self-respecting" mean to you? How do you define it?

For me, it includes being honest with myself, not being critical towards myself, and owning my opinions. It also means being caring and considerate towards myself, and feeling worthy of attention and respect.

On a more practical level, it includes taking the best care of myself that I can (exercising regularly, eating nourishing food, etc.) and surrounding myself with like-minded people.

When you have a strong sense of self-respect, you naturally attract other people who are self-respecting, and who will respect you, too.

Your Tune-Up of the Day:

Today, practice the art of being "self-respecting" ... with a **walking meditation**.

Set aside at least 10 minutes to take a stroll outside.

As you're walking, **say to yourself** (in your mind or out loud, if you can) *"I like and respect myself"*.

Enjoy how this feels. Enjoy how tenderly you're treating yourself. Most of all, enjoy your own company.

If you find yourself thinking negative thoughts or wandering off into other topics, that's OK. Just let those thoughts pass through your mind, like clouds that drift by in the sky.

Once you've completed your walk, find a mirror. Say to your reflection, *"I enjoyed your company and I appreciate you very much."*

If you're unable to take a walk ... you can experience self-respect by doing this exact same exercise while sitting comfortably in a chair, or lying down on a bed. **Just breathe and practice thinking respectful thoughts**. When you're done, find a mirror and express your appreciation.

If you're currently in a relationship ... invite your partner to go on a walking meditation, at the same time. When you both return from your separate walks, share how it felt to practice being self-respecting.

Once both of you have tuned up your self-respect, you'll find that it's much easier to express respect and appreciation for one another, as well.

This wraps up Day 12 of The Love Tune-Up.

I'll "see" you tomorrow for a love lesson on … gratitude.

CHAPTER **13**

Tuning Up Your ... Gratitude

Welcome to Day 13 of The Love Tune-Up.

Today, we're going to focus on **tuning up your ... gratitude**.

An internet search on the power of gratitude, generates an abundance of results, indicating that **it's one of the most vital elements for a happy life, and happy relationships with others**.

This probably isn't a shock. Most of us know that living in a state of gratitude and appreciation "feels good". And most of us are pretty good at expressing our gratitude towards others. ("Thank you!" "Great job!" "You're a wonderful friend!")

But what about expressing gratitude towards ... yourself?

For many people, that's trickier. But **if you want to enjoy relationships with other people that are filled with genuine** gratitude — not "empty praise" or an illusion of appreciation — it's essential to begin with yourself.

Your Tune-Up of the Day:

Today, **find a photograph of you as a small child** — ideally, under 6 years of age. If you don't have one, make a drawing. (Don't worry if it's scribbly or silly!)

For the rest of the day, keep your photo (or drawing) close by, at all times — just like a mother who holds her newborn close to her all the time.

At least 10 times during the course of the day, look at the child in the photograph (or drawing) and say:

"I love you. I accept you. I am so grateful for you. Thank you for being in my life."

Each time you say these words, you are giving the child who lives on inside you (figuratively speaking), an extra dose of love and attention (which you may not have received when you actually were a child).

This is an example of what it means to meet your own "emotional needs" without relying on an external source like a parent, boss, friend or spouse to "fill you up" with good feelings. You can do that, for yourself, all by yourself.

Any additional love and gratitude that you receive from the outside world is just a "bonus" — overflowing your love-cup, instead of filling it up.

This wraps up Day 13 of The Love Tune-Up.

You've done so many exercises, and even though we may not have met face-to-face outside of the pages of this book, I find myself feeling so proud of you. I hope you're feeling proud of yourself, too.

Your love-lessons are over, for now, but as you keep reading, you'll find that **there are a few more surprises in store for you.**

CHAPTER 14

A Few Words of Encouragement

Welcome to Day 14 of The Love Tune-Up.

There's no "lesson" today — **just a few words of encouragement.**

As the playwright and poet Oscar Wilde once wrote:

"To love oneself is the beginning of a lifelong romance."

He's quite right. Friends may drift in and out of your life. Dates can be fun ... or not. Boyfriends and girlfriends may come and go. Spouses, sadly, sometimes leave or pass away.

There is no relationship that is truly, firmly, unquestionably guaranteed to last "forever".

Except your relationship with yourself.

You are your life-long companion. So if you're going to invest time, care and energy into "tuning up" any of your relationships, start by fine-tuning your relationship with yourself.

Once you do, you might just discover that in time, all of your other relationships become sweeter, more rewarding and easier to navigate. Especially if, like we talked about yesterday in your lesson on gratitude, you're operating from a state of overflow — a surplus! — instead of an emotional deficit.

Living in a state of self-love means you'll need less from others, and at the same time, you'll have more to give.

And when you partner up with someone who is operating in the same way?

Now THAT'S true love.

PS. As you know, *The Love Tune-Up* was going to be 14 days long, and it is ... sort of. But I have included a few more surprises for you.

Keep reading ... and enjoy!

WRAP UP

RESOURCES... TO KEEP THE LOVE ROLLING

Your *Love Tune-Up* is "technically" complete, but I wanted to give you some **more resources on self-love, dating, and partnerships** ... in case you'd like to keep the love rolling.

Here are some of my favorites — articles I've authored,[1] Life Guides I've created, a handbook I've written, and insights I shared when I was interviewed by a reporter from the Weekend Today Show, to savor at your leisure.

Enjoy to the fullest ...

---

[1] All articles referenced in this section were published online.

SELF-LOVE

6 Self-Sabotaging Habits You Need To Drop Right Now
— Published on Mind Body Green.
In this article, I encourage readers to do a "habit audit". This means: Paying attention to whether they're sabotaging themselves by being mean to themselves, saying "Yes" when they really mean "No", or blaming their parents for how their life turned out for example,... and to drop these habits if they're present.

https://www.mindbodygreen.com/0-14014/6-selfsabotaging-habits-you-need-to-drop-right-now.html

How Successful People Do More in 24 Hours Than the Rest of Us Do in a Week
— Published on Newsweek.

The content in this article is bound to inspire. Some of the topics I cover include: "Fully Commit," "Ban 'Friendly Interruptions' at All Costs," "Hang With Fellow Super-Achievers," and "Prevent Emotions From Building." It takes a self-loving person to take this type of positive action to further their success.

https://www.newsweek.com/career/how-successful-people-do-more-24-hours-rest-us-do-week

You Are The Best Investment You'll Ever Make
— Published on Dr. Gelb's column, "All Grown Up," on Psychology Today.

In this article, I address ways to invest in ourselves and I present some questions about self-investment practices that readers can reflect on. Readers are encouraged to make a list of doable ways they can invest in themselves. I offer suggestions about what to include on their list.

https://www.psychologytoday.com/blog/all-grown/201511/you-are-the-best-investment-youll-ever-make

If You Want to Make Tomorrow Less Stressful—Start Tonight
— Published in Dr. Gelb's Column, "Be Well At Work," on The Muse.

The stress management tips that I cover in this article, apply to all aspects of life, not just a workday.

This article is a relevant read if you want to learn how to manage your emotions and keep your stress levels in check.

It includes suggestions for stress-relieving activities that take place after-work and an empowering morning affirmation to set the tone for a positive day. You'll also learn about the importance of scheduling deep breathing breaks during the day, and how to do an emotional inventory (and an emotional release, if needed) at the end of the day.

https://www.themuse.com/advice/if-you-want-to-make-tomorrow-less-stressfulstart-tonight

Side note: The Muse is an online platform that attracts more than 75 million people each year, to help them be at the top of their game at work.

I'm honored to have received the praise below, from Adrian Granzella Larssen, Editor-in-Chief, in response to an article that I wrote for The Muse:

"Wow! This is fantastic stuff. You're clearly incredible at what you do, and I'm so thrilled to share your advice with our audience!"

Why "Certain People" Make Us Feel Completely Insane And How To Reclaim Our "Zen."
— Published on Positively Positive.

If you've ever felt really mad when you're around a particular person (you know, the type of anger that can stick around for hours, even when you're no longer in the presence of the person whom you're angry at), this article might be worth a read.

Relationships can be important teachers, bringing to our attention, for example, emotions that we're experiencing that need to be resolved.

That's the focus of this article — how to handle our anger when someone makes us feel annoyed… but where our annoyance is excessive given the situation at hand. I include three questions, along with answers, that can be helpful for people who want to replace being mad around certain people with reclaiming their "zen."

https://bit.ly/2HOCdAg

Welcome Home: Release Addictions and Return to Love
— — Written by Dr. Suzanne Gelb, Ph.D, J.D.

If you're wanting to break free from an addictive habit (from alcoholism to workaholic-ism) and connect to your essence — love — that's what this book is about.

A core message in *Welcome Home* is that with patience and courage, it's possible to learn how to become emotionally self-reliant. That means depending on ourselves, not some external substance, activity, or person, to manage our challenges, and to feel at peace and at home in our lives.

https://amzn.to/2vwXmIa

"Just Believe." How I Learned To Trust In The Universe, Even When All Hope Seemed Lost
— Published in Positively Positive.

This is a true and inspiring article about the importance of believing in yourself … and keeping hope alive … even when the future looks bleak.

http://www.positivelypositive.com/2015/03/26/just-believe-how-i-learned-to-trust-in-the-universe-even-when-all-hope-seemed-lost/

Stressed Out at Work? How to Cope — Without Turning to Food or Booze.
— Originally published on The Huffington Post.

Workplace demands and pressure seems to "come with the territory" in so many instances.

It's no surprise then, that many people routinely try to "escape" this stress by consuming something sweet [lots of it! — say, a pint of ice cream], numbing out with alcohol, or some other pacifier.

A far healthier approach would be to manage work-related stress by relying on one's inner strength. To learn more, including my five stress relief techniques, this article is a must-read.

https://www.huffpost.com/entry/stressed-out-at-work-how_n_6711034

Don't Feel Like Exercising? 3 Steps To Get You Off The Couch
— Published in Dr. Gelb's column, "All Grown Up," on Psychology Today.

We know how good it feels AFTER we've worked out. The problem for many people though, is GETTING MOTIVATED to work out. Sometimes, unresolved emotions "weigh" us down, and dull our desire to work out.

This article offers tips on how to begin to clear out some of the emotional weight that can stop us dead in our tracks, and keep our running shoes in the closet... instead of on our feet!

https://www.psychologytoday.com/blog/all-grown/201505/don-t-feel-exercising-3-steps-get-you-the-couch

5 Ways to Stop Yourself from Eating When You're not Hungry.
— Originally published on Psych Central.

In addition to believing in yourself and your ability to handle life's challenges without the illusory "help" of food [or whatever person, place, or thing, someone might turn to as a coping mechanism], in this article I also lay out five strategies to consider implementing, in an effort to thwart using food [or any addictive substance/behavior for that matter] to cope.

Strategies include: Identifying the real source of hunger (clue: it's not physical), dialoguing with the food, and remembering the downside of eating for the wrong reasons... disappointment afterwards, and physical discomfort.

https://psychcentral.com/blog/5-ways-to-stop-yourself-from-eating-when-youre-not-hungry/

Why Accomplishment Often Leaves Us Feeling Empty: How to heal that longing at last.
— Originally published on The Daily Love — Now published in Dr. Gelb's column, "All Grown Up," on Psychology Today.

Would you believe that the best day of my life was also my worst! That was also the day that I became convinced that earning loads of praise (something I was addicted to) is no substitute for feelings of "self-worth".

And if I had any doubts that eating to soothe my inner emotional void leads me to feel even emptier, not better, on that day my doubts were put to rest, permanently.

Curious how to dig oneself out of this agonizing, addictive cycle? I write about that and more, in this article.

https://www.psychologytoday.com/us/blog/all-grown/201905/why-accomplishment-often-leaves-us-feeling-empty

Why Positive Affirmations Don't Always Work (And What Does)
— Published on Tiny Buddah

In this article, I share how I ultimately figured out why repeated positive affirmations never resulted in lasting transformation for me, personally, and how "affirmations of truth" paved the way for lasting change.

I also offer some examples of what I mean by "affirmations of truth."

http://tinybuddha.com/blog/why-positive-affirmations-dont-always-work-and-what-does/

Aging With Grace, Strength and Self-Love. (A Life Guide)
— Written by Dr. Suzanne Gelb, Ph.D, J.D.

This Life Guide offers a beautiful opportunity to let go of the negativity that so many people carry around about aging, to feel good again, and get back to enjoying life.

In this Guide, you'll learn how to refocus on what brings you joy (a pure act of self-love), how to look forward to all of the pleasures that are yet to come, and lots more. .

https://amzn.to/2VYatSx

"Still Mad at Your Parents? How to Forgive and Move On, Once and for All."
— Published on Positively Positive

In this article, I offer a glimpse into my relationship with my wonderful mom and how I learned to let go of the resentment I felt towards her (and held onto for many years) about my upbringing.

Frankly, for the longest time, I thought I wouldn't be able to forgive her, ever. But I learned that one of the most **self-loving** things I could do for myself, would be to do just that.

http://www.positivelypositive.com/2014/08/07/still-mad-at-your-parents-how-to-forgive-and-move-on-once-and-for-all/

DATING

Navigating Being Single – And Savor Your Dating Adventure. (A Life Guide).

Are you nervous about getting back into the dating pool? Tired of attracting the wrong people? It's possible to learn how to enjoy the dating adventure with this uplifting guide by your side! Includes a series of steps and tools to help you prepare for and build the loving, healthy relationship you deserve.

https://amzn.to/2QKm1CS

Praise for Dr. Gelb's Life Guides

"Dr. Gelb has a gentle spirit that instantly makes you feel like you've come home. The depth of her wisdom is undeniable, her curiosity is insatiable and her love is palpable. These qualities make her the perfect guide for life. In the pages of the Life Guides you will find practical and proven processes to support you in living your great life. Whether it's heart-centered wisdom on navigating the dating world, love-based strategies for becoming a parent, or reaching your ideal weight through kindness, Dr. Gelb's Life Guides are gifts to be treasured."

— Dr. Gemma Stone, Psychologist, Mentor, Author

"Let's be honest: there's a lot of crappy dating advice out there. But Dr. Gelb's Life Guide is a cut above the rest. This is sincere, heart-centered, healthy wisdom that WILL help singles find their special someone."

— Annika Martins, Host of The Sacred Podcast

"Learning how to love yourself and treat yourself kindly — even when your life, career, body, and relationships aren't 'totally perfect' — is one of the hardest things to do. Dr. Suzanne Gelb breaks down the art of self-love into practical steps. No woo-woo vagueness. Just easy-to-follow exercises pulled from her 28-year career in the field. If you're looking for practicality and effectiveness, these Life Guides are a steal of a deal."

— Susan Hyatt, Master Certified Life Coach, Published Author, WebTV Host, International Speaker

Had Your Heart Broken? 21 Reasons To Start Dating Again
— Published on Mind Body Green.

If you're ready to start dating again, but need some encouragement, this article gives you 21 motivating reasons to get back out there... including: Learning to manage rejection differently, enjoying being emotionally available, and knowing that you've learned from the past and can spot red flags more easily.

https://www.mindbodygreen.com/0-15548/had-your-heart-broken-21-reasons-to-start-dating-again.html

4 Ways to Deal With an Office Crush
— Published on The Muse in my column "Be Well At Work".

This article looks at the pros and cons of dating someone at work, and explores factors to keep in mind such as: You are in charge – not your feelings, guilt thoughts cloud our ability to use good judgement, and it's OK to enjoy the excitement of a workplace crush.

https://www.themuse.com/advice/4-ways-to-deal-with-an-office-crush

Side note: The Muse is an award-winning online career resource, with over 4 million quality, professional members. I'm honored to have received the praise below, from Adrian Granzella Larssen, Editor-in-Chief, in response to article that I wrote for The Muse:

"Wow! This is fantastic stuff. You're clearly incredible at what you do, and I'm so thrilled to share your advice with our audience!"

Why I Still Believe People Can Change
— Published on Positively Positive.

Over the course of decades of working in the field of emotional wellness, I've seen so many people release negative emotions and embrace love. That's why I believe people can change... even someone who stopped dating (fear of rejection), but found the confidence to date again and fell-in-love. Read this article to learn more.

http://www.positivelypositive.com/2014/12/15/why-i-still-believe-that-people-can-change/

PARTNERSHIPS

Real Men Don't Vacuum. And Other Misguided Myths That Cause Conflict in Relationships.

I wrote this handbook decades ago (published in 1991, by National Seminars Publications, Inc.). But the information within its pages is timeless: the havoc that unrealistic expectations can wreak on relationships, how to break down barriers to effective communication, and how to constructively minimize tension in a marriage [applies to other relationships, as well] for example — all this, set against a backdrop of dispelling marital myths such as: "Having a Child Can Solve Marital Problems" and "True Lovers Automatically Know Each Other's Thoughts and Feelings".

https://www.amazon.com/Real-Men-Dont-Vacuum-Gelb/dp/B000E5CWWA

How to Rekindle That Spark - and Create The Relationship And Sex Life That You Want. (A Life Guide)

Sex life feeling "blah"? Feeling cold because of something your partner did?

Before heading for divorce court, or having that big break-up talk… learn about my Life Guide on How to Rekindle That Spark — and Create The Relationship & Sex Life That You Want.

Your love is worth one more shot.

https://amzn.to/2WZqKlT

What Readers Are Saying about this Life Guide:

"This Guide got us out of our relationship rut and helped us stir up the passion we felt early on in our relationship, and to remember why we fell in love in the first place.

Thanks to the simple and do-able exercises, we have revived fun, play and touch in our relationship. Hand-holding and hugs used to be a thing of the past. No more!"

—John and Elise

"Before working through this Guide, we were more like roommates who've lived together for years and the romance had gone. Thanks to this Guide we share much more affection and connection, and my lingerie is no longer collecting dust!

We are also more compassionate and kind to each other. And now we schedule time for each other — even if it's for sex. We have to reserve this time, and we look forward to sharing an activity together."

—Rob and Jessie

"We were contemplating divorce. Then we thought we'd 'try one last time' ... so we read your guide. Now? We're best friends again, off-the-top lovers, and totally recommitted.

PS. We're not exaggerating. Dr. Gelb's Life Guide is amazing. It works!"

—Michael and Nadine

Spring Cleaning for Your Life [Part 2/3]
— Published on The Huffington Post.

This article is part of a series on tidying up our inner world – I call this "spring cleaning for your life." It contains a checklist for couples that can add some sizzle and tender closeness to their relationship. Topics on the checklist: "Goals and life direction", "Sex and intimacy", "Forgiveness" and "Self-love".

https://www.huffpost.com/entry/spring-cleaning-for-your-life-part-2-3_n_7271136insight

How to Succeed Everywhere: 10 Tips for Balance at Work, Home, in Relationships
— Written by Shelby Marra, published online on NBC's Today.

Learn my top ten tips on how women [can apply to anyone] can become high achievers in whatever they do — at work, in romance and as a parent. For partners, the romance section in this article, can be especially insightful.

https://www.today.com/health/how-become-high-achieving-woman-work-your-relationship-parent-t33071

Side note: As my colleague, friend, and gifted writing teacher, Alex Franzen said: *"THIS IS AMAZING! Being interviewed by a reporter from NBC's Today Show? Uh, that's the big leagues!"*

Yes, that's what happened. Shelby Marra with NBC's Today Show in New York, requested an interview with me so that she could write this article featuring me, for TODAY.com's Successful Women series.

7 Questions To Ask Before You Start A Rebound Relationship
— Published on Mind Body Green.

Ever ended a relationship, and started a new one almost immediately? And then wondered if you're on the rebound or why you're rushing things? This article poses questions to ask yourself to help identify if you're rebounding. If yes, then you can consider "course correcting" and avoid possible heartache.

https://www.mindbodygreen.com/0-17955/7-questions-to-ask-before-you-start-a-rebound-relationship.html

How To Forgive The One Who Hurt You Most Of All (A Life Guide)
— Written by Dr. Suzanne Gelb, Ph.D, J.D.

If you are feeling weighed down by grief or anger from past fights or betrayals, and want to learn how to forgive, this guide could be a perfect fit.

https://amzn.to/31qPCGq

What readers are saying about this Life Guide:

"I was quite excited to receive your Forgiveness Life Guide and hoped it would help me in healing a particularly intense issue I've been harboring for many years. So far, nothing has worked and I was beyond ready to get this poison out of my life.

This past weekend, I read and thoroughly completed your guide. It was a definite "Aha moment" for me. I felt a tangible, immediate shift in my thinking.

This is no joke nor is it an exaggeration but I now feel more energy, clarity, and excitement than I've felt in ages (think puppy after a bath).

And I'm no longer afraid that the feelings of betrayal might be triggered & resurface because I know I have your guide to get me right back on track.

It was so simple and yet so powerful.

I can't begin to thank you enough."

— Beth

"This guidebook has shown me the difference between natural, healthy, appropriate anger ... and the heavy weight of a grudge. I'm glad that now I know the difference."

— Alexandra Franzen, writing coach, author

You Want Couple's Counseling But Your Partner Does Not
— Published on Psychology Today.

Does this mean you should give up? Not necessarily. In this article, you can learn why your seeking counseling, even if your partner does not, can be of benefit to you, and possibly be positive for your current relationship as well.

https://www.psychologytoday.com/us/blog/all-grown/201504/you-want-couple-s-counseling-your-partner-does-not

What Really Happens in a Therapy Session?
— Published on Psychology Today.

Ever wonder how a therapy session works? 181,223 people have been wondering - they viewed my article on this subject. Topics covered in the article include: Choosing the right therapist, effectiveness of in-person therapy vs. phone or video format, and the value of seeing a therapist vs. talking to friends or family.

https://www.psychologytoday.com/intl/blog/all-grown/201512/what-really-happens-in-therapy-session

Planning a Wedding? A Psychologist's Take on How to Focus on What Matters
— Published on The Huffington Post.

Many people dream of their future wedding day, replaying this special event over and over in their minds. It truly is an exciting day… perhaps one of the best days of a bride and groom's life!

So why is getting married also so stressful for some many couples?

In this article, I offer some tips to dissolve that stress and refocusing on the true significance of one's wedding day… a public commitment to marry the one who you love and adore!

http://www.huffingtonpost.com/dr-suzanne-gelb/planning-a-wedding-planning_b_5464023.html

WHAT'S NEXT?

Remembering to Tune-Up Your Relationship With Yourself and / or Your Partner

Recently, you finished moving through *The Love Tune-Up*: a course on how to build a relationship that really works (… starting with your relationship with yourself).

I know that life is hectic at times, and it can be tough to remember what you had for breakfast this morning — let alone remember the powerful tune-up exercises that you did to create a more loving relationship with yourself and others, days ago!

That's why today, I just wanted to check in and say:

"How's it going?"

- Are you being kind and respectful towards yourself, today?

- If not, why not?

- Is it time for a walk, a few deep breaths, or a few moments of quiet to listen deeply to yourself?

- If you're in a relationship, is it time to express your appreciation for your partner, to listen actively without interrupting, or willingly make a compromise, without resentment?

If you feel inspired to do so — no pressure, whatsoever — you can **do some journaling** (complete the sentence/s below) and/or **reach out to a friend or to a loved one, and tell them:**

Today, I am tuning up my relationship with myself by

_____

_____

_____

_____

And / or:

Today, I am tuning up my relationship with my partner by

_____

_____

_____

I bet there's someone (that includes yourself!) who'd love to hear what you're working on today — and no matter who you choose to tell, be ready for a happy reply.

A FEW FINAL WORDS

HAPPINESS BEGINS NOW, CREATING YOUR TRULY EXCEPTIONAL LIFE, ONE STEP AT A TIME

> *"Take the first step in faith.*
> *You don't have to see the whole staircase, just take the first step."*
> — Dr. Martin Luther King, Jr.

It has been my honor to offer you many beautiful "steps" to take, in the pages of this book.

I hope that these love lessons carry you **higher and higher** up the staircase of happiness.

Closer and **closer** to:

— the **life** you want to have,

— the **relationships** you want to experience

and

— the **person** you want to be.

As Dr. King reminds us,

you don't need all the answers in order to keep making progress.

Just **a willing heart**, and the **desire** to continue.

MORE TIPS, MORE TOOLS

FAQs About How To Find Love — and Stay in Love

Now that you've read all fourteen of the lessons in the *Love Tune-Up*, you know more about what makes a relationship work and about negative habits that can sabotage love. Here are even more tips and tools to continue your journey to become a more self-loving person and enjoy more positive relationships with others.

Read on for my answers[2] to some of the more typical questions I've been asked over the past 3+ decades as I've helped people learn to upgrade their relationships with themselves — and others.

---

[2] The questions and answers are summarized here, to maximize your learning experience.

Question No. 1 — Hiding my true self

Finding the Courage To Be "Me."

"If I didn't know better, I'd be thinking that I was born as a people pleaser.

But I know that I started doing that from an early age, so that people would like me (you can tell that I've read my share of self-help materials!).

But as much as I do affirmations, telling myself, 'It's ok to be me,' when I'm actually on a date (I'm still single, and really want to find the 'right' partner), it's like I have this default switch that kicks in, and I transform into the people-pleaser... saying what I think someone wants to hear. I'm good at figuring that out (I have a life time of experience!).

But that always backfires because it's just a matter of time, in a dating situation, when it gets to the point that I feel stuck in this people-pleasing personality that I've been displaying to my date — and that my date thinks is the real 'Me', — and at that point, it's too late to show my date who the real 'Me' is... and even if it wasn't too late, I don't have the guts to show the real 'Me'.

So then I go back to doing more affirmations to try to be more confident so I can be the real 'Me.' At the time I'm saying these affirmations, I feel hopeful that they will work.

But they don't! And then I feel really down....

Do people get stuck in this vicious cycle? How do they get out of it?"

Response:

Yes, what you're experiencing is something that a lot of people struggle with.

It is possible to become the person that you were **born** to be…

— free from unhealthy fear that prompts unhealthy behavior (such as people-pleasing).

— free to be who your really are.

— filled with love, and wanting to share that love, and to receive love.

— and more.

But as you've found out, over and over again, your approach to affirmations **didn't lift you up** for very long.

In fact, as you shared in your question, when you realized that your affirmations weren't working, you then **felt "really down".**

One compelling reason why **affirmations don't work**, is because invariably:

— these positive statements are competing with the strong emotions that someone is feeling.

Unless those emotions are addressed **directly**, and then **resolved**,

— these feelings tend to **overwhelm** and **dominate** the affirmations.

Generally speaking, this is primarily why the affirmations don't work.

In light of your question, you might find the article that I wrote specifically on this topic, quite helpful. It is published online, on Tiny Buddha, and is called:

Why Positive Affirmations Don't Always Work (And What Does)

http://tinybuddha.com/blog/why-positive-affirmations-dont-always-work-and-what-does/

[Note to reader:

In my response to this question, I also suggested that this person do a Mini Self-Evaluation, similar to the one that you read about in Chapter 5 ("Tuning Up Your ... Ability To Be The Real You") of this book.

I also outlined a guided visualization to Comfort the Inner Child, similar to the visualization that you read about towards the end of Chapter 5.]

Once you've read the article, and completed the Mini Self-Evaluation and the Guided Visualization, you might try to write some new affirmations, with the type of self-honesty that is written about in the article.

For example:

I am frustrated that I don't show the real "Me" to someone that I am dating, but I am learning to soothe my fears. I am learning to do better.

I am sad that I have so much fear about being the real "me," but I am learning to comfort the source of my fear... my inner child. I am learning to do better.

I am scared to show the real "Me," but I am learning to give myself extra love so that I can achieve my goal of being "Me." I am learning to do better.

If you'd like to use the examples above, you can tweak them as you'd like, to suit your particular situation, and / or you can also create new affirmations using the beginning and the end parts of the sample affirmations.

For example:

I am frustrated that

_____

_____

_____

_____

I am learning to do better.

I am scared to

_____

_____

_____

I am learning to do better.

I am sad that

_____

_____

_____

_____

I am learning to do better.

Be patient with yourself,

— as you learn to do better.

Be understanding with yourself,

— as you learn to do better.

Be compassionate towards yourself,

— as you let go of negative behaviors from the past, and begin to step into the person who your truly are.

Question No. 2 — Annoying listener

Becoming Aware of a Bad Listening Habit

"My wife says I have a very annoying habit when she talks. She says I make sounds while she's talking — but before she's finished what she wants to say — as if I understand, and I'm agreeing to, what she's saying, before she's said it.

Then she accuses me of not listening to her because, as she puts it:

'There's no way you can agree with what I'm saying, because I haven't completed my sentence yet!'

Then she accuses me of not listening to her. In my defense, I say:

'No, I am listening. Honestly, I know you have no reason to make this up... so what you're saying must be true, but didn't know I was making those sounds before you finished your sentence.'

She doesn't believe me, and she says things like:

'Give me a break, how can you not know what's coming out of your mouth. You're a grown man. Stop making excuses!'

This sets off a huge fight between us that never gets resolved, because those sounds come out of me (according to my wife) without me even thinking about making those sounds, or indicating that I'm agreeing with what she's saying.

Aside from this, we get along really well, but I don't know how to fix this and I'm worried that it will drive a big wedge in our relationship. Is there a fix for this?"

Response:

Yes, habits can be dismantled (i.e., broken).

Why?

Because…

• a habit is a learned behavior.

You weren't born with this habit of making sounds when listening to someone talk… as if to indicate agreement with that person before they've finished making their point.

And…

• anything that has been learned, can be unlearned…

and then

• relearned in a different way.

So, since you say that your wife has no reason to be making up this behavior of yours that she finds bothersome (i.e., you agree with her before she's finished speaking), the fix is for you to:

— **unlearn** this habit that she finds bothersome.

In other words, you would need to **teach yourself to refrain** from what your wife perceives as your **annoying listening habit**.

How does one unlearn a habit?

First, keep in mind that a habit is typically an **unconscious behavior**. That's why, in your case, you **don't even know** that you're doing it.

At some point in your life, you adopted (started doing) this behavior.

Then, after **repeating** the behavior enough times, it became so **automatic** that you did it **without consciously thinking** about it.

Think about the first time you learned a particular skill (e.g., driving, typing, etc.)

At first, you had to think about every single move you made. Your thought process was

— very **conscious**...

— very **calculated**...

— very **intentional**.

Then,

— after **mastering** the skill,

and

— with a certain amount of **repetition**,

the skill came easily to you.

You **no longer had to think** about every move, so to speak.

Much of what you were doing with regard to the skill had become **automatic**.

That's great when the habit is a **positive** one.

But what if, as in your situation with your wife, the habit is a **negative** one.

How does you bring that behavior back into consciousness again?

Awareness.

Just **setting your intention** to be **aware** of this habit of making sounds, as your wife has described it, is not only a very important first step — but it's a big part of turning this habit around, so to speak — of resolving it.

Without awareness, we tend to stay stuck in our habit.

Awareness, on the other hand, is like shining a light on the habit — so we begin to notice it... we begin to see ourselves in action.

Once we notice ourselves engaging in the undesired / undesirable behavior, then, in time we're likely to be able to begin to:

- **preempt the negative behavior** before it happens...

until we get to the point where...

- we **no longer engage** in the behavior.

It takes

— practice and commitment to undo a habit.

But it can be done.

It takes:

— tenacity and desire to be mindful of a habit until it is resolved.

But it can be done.

And most of all…

It takes self-respect and self-love to be willing to make this effort for ourselves…

to be willing to do what it takes to **disengage** from a negative behavior that:

— **doesn't serve** us…

— is **not in our best interests**…

— **doesn't support our highest good.**

But it can be done.

[Note to reader:

At this point in my response to this spouse, I also suggested that he

— get a journal

and

— ***write*** *about his attempts to listen more attentively in the journal.*

I also encouraged him to:

*— do some **introspection***

and

*— **think** about*

and then

*— **write** about*

*— **where he might have learned** this poor listening habit,*

and

*— **why** he engages in it, in the way he does.*

These suggestions are similar to the ones that I made, and that you read about, in Chapter 6 of this book.

That Chapter is titled, "Tuning Up Your ... Ability To Be a Good Listener.")

If you want to go back and re-read that Chapter (Day 6 of The Love Tune-Up) as a refresher, feel free to do so now.]

Question No. 3 — Feeling resentful

Letting Go of Anger and Embracing Forgiveness

"My wife lost her father to cancer about a year ago. She was close to her dad and she's the type that keeps her feelings to herself... so I don't think she even cried when her dad died. She was very stoic during the entire ordeal.

Our marriage of 10 years had been solid until about 6 months ago when she filed for divorce, out of the blue.

This came as a big shock to me. I love her very much, and I know she must have been going through a lot because of her dad's illness and death...

I tried to be there for her, emotionally and in every way I could, but again, she keeps her feelings to herself, so after a certain point, I gave up asking her how she was feeling, and if there was anything I could do to help. My heart went out to her, but there was nothing I could do for her.

After she filed for divorce, I asked her to go with me to counseling so we could have a professional help us with whatever was bothering her about our marriage, but she didn't want to. She made it clear that she absolutely didn't want to talk about anything.

Then she was notified that there was a mistake (omission) in the divorce papers that she filed, and so they were not processed, and she would have to fix the error and refile the papers.

She never fixed the error or refiled.

So we are still together... still married.

But now I feel this undercurrent of resentment within myself about the fact that she filed for divorce — even though I'm happy that she hasn't refiled. I thought I was "over" the resentment because I just want to focus on the fact that we're still married... and to move forward from there, but sometimes I feel like I can't forgive her for what she did.

I'm not an angry person, and I've never held a grudge against anyone in my life, but I'm a bit worried that I'll never be able to get over how I feel about what she did.

She seems to have put this 'divorce' move behind her, and I very much want to as well...

But honestly, I think that if I was able to forgive and let this whole painful chapter go, I'd feel weak — like what happened didn't really matter... like it was ok for her to file the papers and just discard our marriage with the stroke of a pen.

(It would be like forgiving my parents for being so relentlessly critical of me when I was growing up. I'd feel weak if I did that — almost like I'd be saying, "It's OK that you were so mean to me for all those years...")

How can that be right?

How can what my wife did be right?

Is it really possible to make peace with what she did?

Response:

I'm happy for you — and for your wife — that she did not file the divorce papers for a second time, because it sounds like you care for her very deeply. I sincerely hope that the two of you will be able to work things out.

Fortunately, one problem that can be worked out, is the problem that you are experiencing within yourself — **resentment**... and also your **reluctance to forgive**.

Forgiveness is not a sign of weakness.

It is

- **an act of pure self-love.**

It is

- **a willingness to relieve yourself of carrying a heavy burden that is carried by you alone — resentment.**

Forgiving someone doesn't mean that:

— what that person did was OK...

or that

— they can do it again...

or that

— what they did is now forgotten.

Forgiving someone means that:

— you give yourself permission to let go of the angry burden that's been festering inside you.

Forgiving your wife means that:

— you're able to **access your own inner emotional strength** such that you can recognize and accept your wife's limitations.

At the time she filed the divorce papers, your wife was **not able to access her own inner emotional strength** that could have supported her in not filing for divorce, until she had first talked it over with you, for example.

Forgiving your wife means that:

— you're able to wake up in the morning feeling:

— **light**

and

— **free**,

rather than:

— heavy

and

— burdened.

[Note to reader:

At this point in my response to this question, I suggested that this spouse write a letter to his wife, in which he expresses his resentment and anger about what she did.

I emphasized that this letter was for his <u>personal use only</u>, and as such, it should <u>never</u> to be sent to his wife.

I explained that the purpose of writing the letter was to create a safe, confidential vehicle through which he could begin to release his pent-up emotions that appeared to be 'standing in the way,' so to speak, of his ability to attain inner peace.

*This **letter-writing exercise** is similar to the one that you read about in Chapter 9 ("Tuning Up Your ... Ability to Forgive and Let Go of Resentment") of this book.*

*I also introduced him to the **pillow-pounding exercise** that was also included in Chapter 9 of this book, in the event that after writing his confidential letter, he felt that he needed to discharge even more anger.*

If you'd like to take a moment to go back and review Chapter 9, and reacquaint yourself with the two exercises noted above, feel free to do so right now.]

Also, since you mentioned that you have not forgiven your parents for being mean to you, you might want to read the article that I wrote on this subject.

It's published online on Positively Positive, and is called:

"Still Mad at Your Parents? How to Forgive and Move On, Once and for All."

http://www.positivelypositive.com/2014/08/07/still-mad-at-your-parents-how-to-forgive-and-move-on-once-and-for-all/

It's not uncommon for adults to have difficulty forgiving someone with whom they have a relationship (e.g., a spouse), because of unresolved resentment that is **unrelated** to this current relationship.

Instead, the pent-up emotions are rooted in another relationship(s), typically from an earlier time (e.g., a relationship with a parent or caregiver.)

This is why

it is wise, when trying to forgiving someone, to do a self-inventory and take stock of:

- **whether there is anyone else that you need to forgive, as well...**

- **whether there is another relationship that needs healing, as well...**

Otherwise, what tends to happen is that people have difficulty totally letting go of resentment that they feel towards someone, no matter how hard they try to let go of it.

A commonly occurring reason why the resentment may linger, is because instead of realizing that the resentment is connected to

more than one relationship, the person who is holding a grudge and having difficulty forgiving, thinks that their **all** of their resentment is related to only one person ... only one relationship (in your case, that would be your relationship with you wife.)

But only when they:

— **realize** that not **all** of the resentment they are feeling is connected solely to one relationship,

and only when they:

— **resolve** their resentment to **all** of their relationships in which resentment is connected, (no matter how long ago these relationships might have occurred, e.g., childhood),

Will they be able to begin to:

— **enjoy** inner peace and freedom from pent-up resentment.

In this article, you'll also find an example of a letter of forgiveness. You may want to give it a try.

Doing this letter-writing exercise could be a good compliment to other letter-writing exercise that I suggested earlier, in which you release your pent-up feelings, safely and confidentially.

As with the first letter-writing exercise, this second letter of forgiveness is **for your eyes only**. It is **not** to be read by anyone, except you.

Finally, if you want to learn even more about how to forgive, take a look at the Life Guide that I wrote on this topic.

How To Forgive The One Who Hurt You Most Of All (A Life Guide).

https://amzn.to/31qPCGq

Question No. 4 — Sad divorcee

Learning From Past Mistakes

"I recently got divorced. We were only married for a short time but I really thought things were going to work out because when we were dating, I thought he was my lifetime partner, for sure!

But even right after our honeymoon, things started to fall apart. He started saying things to me that made no sense... like,

'That was the lousiest vacation I've ever had, I'll make sure that never happens again!'

That comment took me by surprise because I thought we had a really good time — but evidently he didn't.

After that, we just had one clash after another. Like, we started arguing about money, and how much time we would spend with each other's family, and just about everything you could think of.

I felt completely blind-sided and kept replaying in my mind a tormenting question:

'How could I have made such a colossal mistake? What's wrong with me?'

In hindsight, there was so much that we didn't know about each other before we committed to each other... there were so many things we didn't talk about and obviously needed to...

Now I wonder how could I have avoided this gigantic failure? I'd like to get married again someday, but how can I avoid another failed relationship?"

Response:

I'm sorry things didn't work out the way you wanted them to.

But don't lose hope.

The beautiful thing about life is that we can learn from our past, and grow stronger and wiser because of that.

It sounds like you've identified **the root of the problem** — a lack of really getting to know each other and establishing compatibility, **before** you decided to "tie the knot."

As you said:

"...there was so much that we didn't know about each other before we committed to each other... there were so many things we didn't talk about and obviously needed to..."

The lesson:

For relationships to have any type of a lasting future … any type of longevity, **compatibility** must be firmly established.

This means:

— Two people spending quality time together… talking about their dreams, goals, values, priorities, hopes, desires, etc.

This means:

— Doing simple things together, like going shopping together, watching the sunset together, having a meal together (without the distraction of television or any other electronic devices).

There's no **one-size-fits-all** script or protocol in terms of **steps to take to get to know someone**, and / or what to talk about or discuss to achieve this goal, because every person is unique and, as such, every relationship is unique.

Generally speaking, it's really about a choice to:

— spend **meaningful** time with someone,

— be **fully present** as you do so,

— share **the "real" you**

— **listen** attentively,

and:

— **pay attention** to how this person relates to you and to others when you're with them,

and

— how **you feel** when you're with this person.

Keep in mind that:

It takes time to get to know someone.

So it's important to:

- **not rush into things.**

It's also important to be able to trust your ability to:

- **properly assess the merits of your dating / relationship experience**

and to:

- **determine whether there truly is compatibility (and therefore a future) with someone.**

If you feel like you could use some support with being able to trust your ability to assess and determine compatibility, or perhaps you just want to brush up on these abilities, then you might consider reaching out to a qualified professional for some additional support.

But most of all,

— be **kind** to yourself as you heal from this loss.

— be **patient** with yourself as you learn from past choices.

— be **encouraging** to yourself about new beginnings in the future.

ABOUT THE AUTHOR

Dr. Suzanne Gelb, Ph.D., J.D. is a psychologist, life coach, relationship expert and author. Over the past 30+ years, she has spent 1000s of hours helping people to upgrade and optimize their relationships, using tools like the ones in this book.

Dr. Gelb's expert insights on personal growth have been featured on more than 200 radio programs, 200 TV interviews, and online on Time, Newsweek, Forbes, The Huffington Post, NBC's Today, Psychology Today, The Daily Love, Positively Positive, Mind Body Green, The Muse and many other places, as well.

She is the author of several other books on relationships including **How to Rekindle That Spark… & Create the Relationship & Intimacy That You Want**, **How To Forgive The One Who Hurt You Most Of All**, and **Real Men Don't Vacuum. And Other Misguided Myths That Cause Conflict in Relationships**.

Helping people to find love — and stay in love — is one of Dr. Gelb's absolute favorite things in the world. She believes that it is never too late to become the person — and partner — you want to be. Strong. Confident. Calm. Creative. Free of all of the burdens that have held you back — no matter what has happened in the past.

To learn more, visit DrSuzanneGelb.com.

OTHER BOOKS BY THE AUTHOR

How to Rekindle That Spark and Create the Relationship and Sex Life That You Want. (A Life Guide)

How to Forgive the One Who Hurt You Most. (A Life Guide)

How To Navigate Being Single — And Savor Your Dating Adventure. (A Life Guide)

Real Men Don't Vacuum. And Other Misguided Myths That Cause Conflict in Relationships.

How to Deal With People Who Drive You Absolutely Nuts. (A Life Guide)

Welcome Home: Release Addiction and Return to Love.

How To Care for Yourself — When You're A Caregiver For Someone Else. (A Life Guide)

How to Reach Your Ideal Weight Through Kindness, Not Craziness. (A Life Guide)

How to Find Work That You Love When You're Stuck in a Job That You Hate. (A Life Guide)

It Starts With You – How To Raise Happy, Successful Children by Becoming the Best Role-Model You Can Possibly Be. A Guidebook For Parents.

How to Get Your Kids to Cooperate and Help Them Become the Best Grown-Ups They Can Be. (A Life Guide)

Helping Your Teen Make Healthy Choices About Dating and Intimacy. (A Life Guide)

How To Get Ready To Be a Parent — and Be the Best Mom or Dad You Can Possibly Be. (A Life Guide)

Aging With Grace, Strength and Self-Love. (A Life Guide)

INDEX[3]

A

admiration, 16
affirmations, 31, 56, 57, 73-76
appreciation, 43-46, 68
anger, 13, 19, 28, 35-37, 53, 64, 65, 84, 88
assumptions, 24
attention, 8, 42, 46, 51, 53, 93
attract, 16, 43

B

biases, 24
breathe, 24, 28, 43

C

calm, 28, 95
care, 8, 19, 37, 42, 49, 86, 96
change, 12, 19, 24, 31, 32, 56, 60
comfort, 22, 75-76
comfortable, 27, 28
commitment, 9, 13, 25, 66, 82
compromise, 9, 19, 26-28, 68
comforting, 22

conflict, 9, 26, 61, 95, 96
couple(s), 1, 5, 7, 9, 12, 63, 66
conversation, 5, 22, 24
co-workers, 11

D

differences, 26
disappointed, 13, 30, 34

E

encouragement, 48, 59
emotional needs, 32, 46
emotionally-whole, 16, 19
expectations, 30-32, 39, 61

F

family, 11, 66, 91
fears, 22, 75
flexible, 30
forgive, 12, 33-35, 40, 57, 64, 85, 86, 88-90, 95, 96
forgiveness, 12, 32, 63, 64, 84, 86, 90
friends, 11, 31, 48, 62, 66

---

[3] The page numbers in this index refer to the printed version of this book.

frustration, 31

G

good listener, 8, 18, 23, 83
grudge, 12, 65, 85, 90
gratitude, 44-46, 49

H

habits, 11, 13, 19, 25, 51, 72, 79
happier, 6, 17,
happiness, 31, 70
happy, 3, 4, 6-9, 12, 16-19, 21, 33, 35, 45, 69, 85, 86, 96
healing, 34, 64, 89
healthier, 13, 54

I

inner child, 22, 75, 76
insight(s), 10, 28, 50, 95
interrupt, 24
interrupting, 680
irritation, 31

J

journaling, 5, 9, 25, 37, 68

K

kindness, 16, 17, 58, 96

L

life-long companion, 49
life of love, 40
like-minded people, 42
limitations, 17, 87
listen, 24, 25, 40, 68, 83, 93
listening, 8, 23-25, 78, 79, 83
listening skills, 8, 23
love contract, 40, 41
love-sabotaging habits, 11, 13, 19

M

mind-read, 24
myths about compromise, 27
mistakes, 12, 91

N

negative habit(s) 11, 13, 72

O

overreact, 24
open mind, 24

P

passive-aggressive, 36
patient, 40, 77, 94

peace, 27, 35-37, 54, 85, 88, 90
partner, 4, 5, 8, 12, 17, 25-26, 31, 36, 43, 49, 50, 61, 65, 67, 68, 73, 91, 95
partnerships, 11, 50, 61
priority, 9
problem-diverter, 26
problems, 9, 30, 61

R

"the real you", 21
reflect, 17, 18, 25, 28, 51
resentment, 12, 19, 28, 33, 34, 57, 68, 85, 86, 88-90
respect, 4, 8, 16, 17, 19, 28, 40, 42-44
respectful, 28, 37, 43, 67
romantic, 11

S

sabotaging, 11, 13, 19, 51
selective listening, 24
self-evaluation, 21
self-love, 17, 39, 49-51, 57, 59, 63, 82, 86, 97
self-love inventory, 17

self-respect(ing), 4, 27, 42-44, 82
sensitivity, 16, 17
single(s), 5, 9, 58, 73, 96
strength, 34, 54, 57, 87, 97
stress, 13, 52, 54, 66
support, 12, 32, 58, 82, 94

T

true love, 4, 49
true self, 8, 21, 27, 73

U

uncertainty, 15
understood, 8
unloving, 40
unkind, 16, 39

V

validated, 8

W

walking meditation, 43
worthy, 16, 42
writing, 10, 19, 37, 88

www.ingramcontent.com/pod-product-compliance
Lightning Source LLC
Chambersburg PA
CBHW020144130526
44591CB00030B/200